Chisinau Travel Guide 2025

"Explore Moldova's Vibrant Capital: Hidden Gems, Culture, Cuisine & Day Trips Beyond the City"

David Pike

Copyright © [David Pike] 2025. All Rights Reserved

Before this document can be legally duplicated or reproduced in any manner, the publisher's consent must be gained. Therefore, the contents within this document can neither be stored electronically, transferred, nor kept in a database. Neither in part, nor in full can this document be copied, scanned, faxed, or retained without approval from the publisher or creator.

Table of Contents

Map of Chisinau	6
Chapter 1: Welcome to Moldova's Capital	**7**
A Brief History of Chisinau	7
Understanding Chisinau's Culture and People	7
Practical Information for Your Trip	7
Chapter 2: Planning Your Chisinau Adventure	**15**
Best Times to Visit Chisinau	15
Visa Requirements and Entry Procedures	17
Budgeting for Your Trip	19
Chapter 3: Getting To and Around Chisinau	**22**
Arriving by Air, Land, and Rail	24
Public Transportation Options	24
Renting a Car and Driving in Chisinau	24
Chapter 4: Discovering Chisinau's Landmarks	**28**
The Grand National Assembly Square	28
The Nativity Cathedral	30
The Triumphal Arch	32
Chapter 5: Immersing Yourself in Culture	**33**
The National Museum of History of Moldova	33
The National Museum of Ethnography and Natural History	35
The National Theatre of Opera and Ballet	37
Chapter 6: Strolling Through Chisinau's Parks and Gardens	**40**
Stefan cel Mare Central Park	40
Valley of Roses Park (Valea Trandafirilor)	43

Botanical Garden	45
Chapter 7: Uncovering Hidden Gems	**47**
Exploring the Old Town Area	47
Discovering Local Markets	50
Architectural Highlights Beyond the Center	52
Chapter 8: Venturing into Moldova's Wine Country 54	
Visiting Cricova Winery	54
Exploring Milestii Mici Winery	56
Other Notable Wine Tours	58
Chapter 9: Day Trips to Historical Sites	**60**
Orheiul Vechi Archaeological Complex	60
Tipova Monastery	62
Soroca Fortress	64
Chapter 10: Exploring Nature and Outdoors	**66**
Condrita Monastery and Surroundings	66
Capriana Monastery and Forests	68
Hiking and Nature Trails Near Chisinau	70
Chapter 11: Accommodation Options in Chisinau	**72**
Hotels and Guesthouses	72
Apartment Rentals	74
Budget-Friendly Choices	76
Chapter 12: Dining and Nightlife	**78**
Traditional Moldovan Cuisine	78
International Dining Options	80
Bars, Pubs, and Clubs	82
Chapter 13: Shopping in Chisinau	**84**
Souvenirs and Local Crafts	84

Modern Shopping Centers	86
Market Experiences	88
Chapter 14: Essential Information and Resources	**90**
Emergency Contacts and Useful Numbers	90
Internet Access and Communication	92
Local Customs and Etiquette	94
Index	**96**

Map of Chisinau

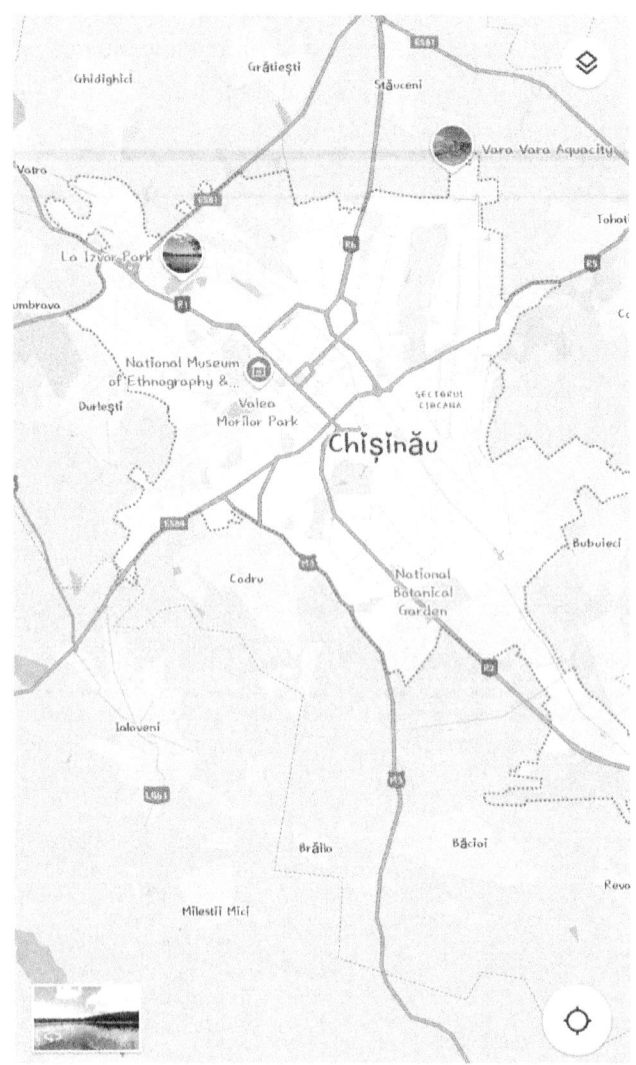

Chapter 1: Welcome to Moldova's Capital

A Brief History of Chisinau

Understanding Chisinau's Culture and People

Practical Information for Your Trip

Chisinau, the capital and cultural heart of Moldova, has a long and layered history that reflects the resilience, spirit, and diversity of its people. Tracing its roots back to the 15th century, Chisinau began as a modest monastic village founded around 1436. Situated on the banks of the Bîc River, it grew slowly under the Principality of Moldavia, maintaining a primarily agrarian identity for centuries. Its name is believed to originate from the archaic Romanian word "chisla" (spring) and "nouă" (new), suggesting "new spring," which likely referred to a water source that played a vital role in the early settlement's survival.

By the early 19th century, the trajectory of the city changed dramatically. Following the Russo-Turkish War, the Treaty of Bucharest in 1812 transferred control of Bessarabia, including Chisinau, from the Ottoman Empire to the Russian Empire. Under Russian rule, Chisinau underwent significant transformation. It expanded rapidly, drawing architectural influence from Russian neoclassicism and baroque styles, while its infrastructure improved to reflect its growing administrative and economic importance. By the end of the 19th century, it had evolved into a bustling provincial center, home to a diverse population of Romanians, Russians, Jews, Ukrainians, and others.

The 20th century brought profound upheaval. After the collapse of the Russian Empire during World War I, Bessarabia united with Romania in 1918, making Chisinau part of Greater Romania. This era brought Romanian influence in education, culture, and administration, but peace was short-lived. The Molotov-Ribbentrop Pact between Nazi Germany and the Soviet Union in 1939 resulted in Soviet occupation in 1940. A year later, the Axis powers occupied the city, leading to widespread devastation and the tragic persecution of the local Jewish population. Soviet forces reoccupied Chisinau in 1944, and it remained under

Soviet control until Moldova declared independence in 1991 following the dissolution of the USSR.

Post-independence, Chisinau has faced numerous challenges, from economic instability to political transitions, yet it has steadily redefined itself as a dynamic European capital. Today, its urban landscape reveals a tapestry of influences: Soviet-era apartment blocks, neoclassical government buildings, leafy boulevards, and modern glass-and-steel constructions—all coexisting within a city that remembers its past while looking resolutely toward the future.

Chisinau's culture is a reflection of its multifaceted history and the rich ethnic mosaic of its inhabitants. The population is predominantly Moldovan (ethnic Romanians), but one can also find significant Russian, Ukrainian, Gagauz, Bulgarian, and Jewish communities. This diversity is not only evident in demographics but also deeply embedded in the city's languages, cuisine, religious practices, and social norms. Romanian is the official language and the most widely spoken, though Russian remains a common lingua franca, especially among older generations and in certain neighborhoods.

Traditional Moldovan values emphasize hospitality, community, and family. Guests are often treated with warmth and generosity, and sharing meals is a central aspect of social interaction. In Chisinau, this cultural emphasis on hospitality is palpable in both informal and formal settings—from being invited to a homemade feast in a local household to the attentiveness of service in family-run restaurants.

Religious faith also plays a significant role in everyday life. The majority of Chisinau's population adheres to Eastern Orthodox Christianity, which is reflected in the city's numerous churches and monasteries. These sites are not only places of worship but also living embodiments of national heritage. Religious holidays, particularly Easter and Christmas, are celebrated with fervor and rich traditions, often blending Orthodox customs with older, pre-Christian folk rituals.

Cultural expression flourishes in Chisinau's thriving arts scene. The city is home to a number of theaters, including the National Theatre Mihai Eminescu and the National Opera and Ballet Theatre, where local talent brings classical and contemporary productions to life. Music, particularly folk and classical, holds a special place in Moldovan culture, and festivals throughout the year celebrate everything from national heritage to wine and gastronomy. Additionally, the city's museums, such as the National Museum of History and the National Museum of Ethnography and Natural History, provide vital insight into the evolution of Moldovan identity.

The social life of Chisinau is increasingly shaped by a younger generation that is globally connected yet deeply rooted in local traditions. This generational bridge manifests in everything from the city's fashion and art scenes to the growing number of coffeehouses, tech startups, and creative spaces. The fusion of old and new gives Chisinau a character that is at once nostalgic and progressive.

For those planning a trip to Chisinau, there are several practical considerations that can greatly enhance the experience. Moldova has a relatively straightforward visa policy. Citizens from the EU, the US, Canada, and many other countries do not require a visa for short stays (usually up to 90 days). However, travelers are advised to verify current entry requirements with their nearest Moldovan consulate or embassy, as policies can change.

The main point of entry into Chisinau is through the Chisinau International Airport, located roughly 13 kilometers southeast of the city center. Taxis, ride-hailing apps, and shuttle buses make the journey into town easy and relatively inexpensive. For those entering by land, buses and trains connect Chisinau with major cities in neighboring Romania and Ukraine. The central railway station and bus terminal are well-situated within the city, providing convenient access to public transportation.

Chisinau's public transport system consists primarily of trolleybuses, minibuses (locally known as "rutieras"), and buses. Trolleybuses are an efficient and affordable way to get around, and tickets can be purchased onboard for a modest fee. While English is increasingly spoken, especially among younger residents and in hospitality venues, a basic knowledge of Romanian or Russian can be very helpful for navigating transport and interacting with locals. Street signs and public notices are mostly in

Romanian, with Russian often appearing as a secondary language.

The Moldovan leu (MDL) is the official currency, and it's advisable to exchange money at official exchange points or withdraw local currency from ATMs, which are widely available in Chisinau. Credit cards are accepted in many hotels, restaurants, and shops, but it's wise to carry some cash for smaller establishments or market stalls.

When it comes to accommodation, Chisinau offers a broad spectrum of options, from luxury hotels and boutique guesthouses to short-term rental apartments and budget-friendly hostels. It's recommended to book accommodations in advance, especially during festival seasons or national holidays, when demand can spike.

Healthcare in Chisinau is adequate for most travelers' needs, though it may not match the standards of Western Europe in terms of facilities or services. Pharmacies are easy to find, and many have staff who can speak English or Russian. Travelers should consider purchasing travel insurance that includes coverage for medical expenses. It's also a good idea to bring any necessary medications with a prescription and their generic names, as brand availability may vary.

Safety in Chisinau is generally not a major concern. The city is considered safe for tourists, though standard precautions should always be taken—particularly at night or in less populated areas. Pickpocketing can occur in crowded places such as markets or public transport, so it's wise to keep belongings secure and avoid displaying valuables.

Chisinau has a temperate continental climate, with warm summers and cold winters. Spring and early autumn are particularly pleasant, offering mild temperatures and vibrant colors in the city's many parks and gardens. It's advisable to pack appropriate seasonal clothing and always check the weather forecast before your trip.

Electricity runs on 220 volts, and the standard plug types are C and F, which are common across Europe. Travelers from countries with different plug types or voltage standards should bring suitable adapters or converters. Internet access is reliable in most parts of Chisinau, with many hotels, cafes, and restaurants offering free Wi-Fi. SIM cards for local mobile networks can be easily purchased, offering affordable data and call packages.

Understanding local customs can go a long way in ensuring a respectful and enjoyable visit. Moldovans tend to be formal in public but warm and open in private settings. Handshakes are a common form of greeting, and addressing people by their titles or surnames is considered polite, particularly in professional contexts. When invited into someone's home, it is customary to bring a small gift, such as flowers, wine, or chocolates. Visitors are also encouraged to dress modestly when entering religious sites and to observe quiet respect during services or ceremonies.

As a destination, Chisinau offers a rewarding mix of history, hospitality, and cultural depth. Its compact size makes it easy to navigate, yet its layered identity invites deep exploration. For the curious traveler, it presents an opportunity not only to see a lesser-known European capital but also to engage with a people and a place that embody both resilience and renewal.

Chapter 2: Planning Your Chisinau Adventure

Best Times to Visit Chisinau

Visa Requirements and Entry Procedures

Budgeting for Your Trip

Chisinau reveals itself most vividly through its changing seasons, each one offering a distinct atmosphere, rhythm, and palette of experiences. While the city can be visited year-round, the best time to immerse oneself in its culture, natural beauty, and dynamic city life depends greatly on the type of experience a traveler seeks. For those drawn to mild weather and blooming landscapes, spring—from late April to early June—presents an ideal window. During this time, the city's parks and boulevards awaken with vibrant blossoms, and the temperature hovers comfortably between 15°C and 25°C. The capital becomes a canvas of color, and locals, liberated from the chill of winter, spend time outdoors, filling cafes, terraces, and public spaces with a relaxed, joyful energy.

Summer in Chisinau, stretching from June through August, offers long, sun-drenched days, ideal for exploring the city's gardens, open-air events, and winery tours in the surrounding countryside. Temperatures can occasionally climb above 30°C, but the abundance of shaded parks and tree-lined avenues provides a welcome reprieve. The warm evenings often bring with them outdoor concerts, festivals, and lively gatherings in the central plazas. However, this season can also bring brief but intense thunderstorms, so packing light, breathable clothing alongside an umbrella or light raincoat is wise.

Autumn, particularly from September to mid-October, is a favorite among many seasoned travelers. It's harvest season in Moldova, which means the markets overflow with fresh produce, and vineyards are at their most active. This is also the time of year when Moldova celebrates National Wine Day, an exuberant weekend festival that highlights the country's viticultural heritage with tastings, performances, and tours. The city takes on a golden hue as trees turn shades of amber and crimson, and the cooler temperatures—usually ranging between

10°C and 20°C—make for pleasant strolls through Chisinau's historic streets and gardens.

Winter, from December through February, casts a quieter, more contemplative mood over the city. Temperatures often fall below freezing, and snow is common, transforming Chisinau into a picturesque winter landscape. While some attractions may operate on limited schedules, the festive season brings its own charm. Christmas markets, twinkling lights, and cultural performances imbue the city with a warm, nostalgic atmosphere. For those who appreciate off-the-beaten-path travel with fewer crowds and lower prices, winter can be an appealing time to visit, especially around the Orthodox Christmas and New Year celebrations, which follow the Julian calendar and are observed in early January.

Entry into Moldova is generally straightforward for most travelers, though specific requirements depend on nationality and purpose of visit. Citizens from the European Union, United States, Canada, United Kingdom, Switzerland, Japan, South Korea, and many other countries are permitted to enter visa-free for tourism purposes, typically for stays up to 90 days within a 180-day period. Travelers should ensure that their passport is valid for at least six months beyond the intended period of stay. Although no visa is required for many nationalities, border officials may request proof of accommodation, onward travel plans, and sufficient funds for the duration of the visit.

For visitors from countries that do require a visa, applications can often be submitted online or at the nearest Moldovan consulate or embassy. Moldova offers an eVisa system that simplifies the process, allowing applicants to upload required documents—such as travel itineraries, hotel bookings, and proof of travel insurance—and receive approval electronically. Processing times are typically swift, though it's advisable to apply at least two to three weeks before travel to account for any delays.

Upon arrival, travelers may be asked to complete an entry form and declare the purpose of their visit. Moldovan border control is generally efficient and courteous, but having a printed or digital copy of hotel reservations and a return ticket can expedite the process. For those entering by land from neighboring countries like Romania or Ukraine, it's important to note that Moldova is not part of the Schengen Area, so separate border controls and customs procedures apply. Visitors planning to enter the breakaway region of Transnistria should also be aware that it has its own informal border checks, and while travel there is usually unproblematic, it's essential to register with Moldovan authorities within 24 hours of entering the country from that region.

Financial planning for a trip to Chisinau involves understanding both the value of the local currency and the relative affordability of the city. Moldova remains one of Europe's most budget-friendly destinations, making it attractive for travelers who seek rich cultural experiences without high costs. The official currency is the Moldovan leu (MDL), and it's best to carry some local cash for small purchases, as not all establishments accept cards, particularly in markets, rural areas, or older cafes.

Daily expenses in Chisinau are generally low compared to Western Europe. Accommodation ranges from luxury hotels and boutique guesthouses to affordable hostels and apartment rentals. A comfortable mid-range hotel room often costs between $40 to $80 per night, while budget travelers can find hostels or simple lodgings for as little as $10 to $20 per night. For longer stays, serviced apartments provide excellent value, especially for families or digital nomads.

Dining is one of Chisinau's greatest pleasures, and it doesn't require a lavish budget. A meal at a traditional Moldovan restaurant, complete with soup, main course, dessert, and wine, can cost as little as $10 to $15 per person. Street food and casual eateries offer filling options like placinta (savory pastries), grilled meats, and stews at even lower prices. International cuisine, including Italian, Turkish, Japanese, and Georgian fare, is widely available, with a mix of upscale and modest venues to suit every wallet.

Transportation within the city is both accessible and economical. Public trolleybuses and buses charge less than 5 MDL per ride, while minibuses cost slightly more but cover additional routes. Taxis and ride-sharing services like Yandex Go are inexpensive and reliable, with most city rides costing under $5. Renting a car is possible, though not necessary for those staying within Chisinau. For excursions into the countryside or wine regions, car hire with or without a driver is readily available and affordable.

Attractions and cultural sites offer a good return on investment for curious visitors. Entrance fees to museums, galleries, and historic buildings are typically modest, often between 20 and 50 MDL. Some outdoor landmarks, like parks and monuments, are free to explore, while others, like guided winery tours or day trips to Orheiul Vechi, can be arranged through local tour operators for reasonable prices. English-speaking guides can be booked for private or group tours, and their services are well worth the cost for those seeking deeper context and storytelling.

For shopping and souvenirs, travelers will find everything from handcrafted ceramics and embroidered textiles to locally made wines and artisanal chocolates. Moldova's wine, in particular, is world-class and attractively priced. Markets like the Central Market (Piata Centrala) or souvenir stalls near major tourist spots offer the chance to haggle for unique gifts while practicing basic Romanian or Russian.

It's wise to factor in additional costs for travel insurance, which is strongly recommended to cover health issues, trip cancellations, or lost baggage. Health care in Chisinau is accessible, with pharmacies and clinics throughout the city, but international visitors may prefer private clinics that offer services in English. Insurance with medical coverage ensures peace of mind, especially for those with existing health conditions or plans to engage in outdoor activities.

Connectivity is affordable and strong in urban Moldova. SIM cards with generous data packages are available from local providers such as Moldcell or Orange for a few dollars. These can be purchased at the airport or local shops with a passport for registration. Free Wi-Fi is common in hotels, restaurants, and public areas, making it easy to stay connected or work remotely if needed.

Ultimately, budgeting for a trip to Chisinau is flexible, with options to suit every traveler. Whether indulging in the comforts of high-end stays and gourmet dining or discovering the city's layers through street food and public parks, the experience is accessible and authentic. The cost-to-experience ratio is exceptionally favorable, allowing for deeper engagement with the culture and landscape without financial strain. Thoughtful preparation and understanding of local customs and logistics can make the journey not only smoother but also far more enriching.

Chapter 3: Getting To and Around Chisinau

Arriving by Air, Land, and Rail

Public Transportation Options

Renting a Car and Driving in Chisinau

Chisinau, the capital of Moldova, welcomes travelers from across the globe with a range of arrival options that suit diverse budgets and itineraries. Whether entering by air, overland, or rail, the journey into the city offers a first glimpse into Moldova's evolving infrastructure and the welcoming character of its people.

For most international visitors, arrival begins at Chisinau International Airport, located about 13 kilometers southeast of the city center. This modernized facility serves as the primary gateway to the country and has been gradually expanding its capacity and amenities in recent years. A growing number of European airlines, including low-cost carriers and full-service operators, connect Chisinau with major cities such as Vienna, London, Istanbul, Rome, Warsaw, and Frankfurt. Additionally, several routes from the Middle East and other regions of Eastern Europe provide options for both leisure and business travelers. The airport itself is compact but efficient, with clear signage in multiple languages and a customs process that is generally smooth. Upon landing, passengers are greeted by a recently refurbished terminal that includes cafes, duty-free shops, currency exchange counters, car rental desks, and free Wi-Fi zones.

Transportation from the airport into the city is convenient and relatively fast. Taxis are readily available just outside the arrivals terminal, with clearly marked official vehicles that operate with meters. Although fares are affordable by European standards, it is recommended to confirm the approximate price before departure or to use a ride-hailing service like Yandex Go or Bolt for a set fare. These apps are widely used in Chisinau and typically provide a more transparent pricing structure. For budget-conscious travelers, an airport bus service operates between the terminal and the central bus station, with scheduled departures throughout the day. This service is reliable and efficient, although it may involve some waiting and limited space for luggage during peak hours.

For those arriving by land, Moldova shares borders with Romania and Ukraine, offering overland entry through a network of well-trafficked crossings. Road conditions have seen considerable improvements in recent years, particularly on the main routes leading into Chisinau. International bus services link the capital with major Romanian cities such as Bucharest, Iasi, and Galati, as well as with cities in Ukraine like Odessa and Kyiv. These long-distance buses are generally modern, air-conditioned, and affordably priced, with several departures per day. The central bus station in Chisinau serves as the hub for international and domestic routes alike, and it is conveniently located within walking distance of the city center. Tickets can be purchased online, at station kiosks, or directly from the driver, although advance booking is advisable during holidays and high travel seasons.

Train travel into Chisinau remains an appealing option for those seeking a more relaxed, scenic route. The city's main railway station, Gara Feroviară, is a grand, Soviet-era structure that still captures the nostalgic charm of train journeys from decades past. While Moldova's rail infrastructure has not undergone the same rapid modernization as its roadways, it continues to function well for international connections, particularly with Romania. Daily trains connect Chisinau with Bucharest, and although the journey is relatively slow, it offers an authentic and contemplative experience of the Moldovan and Romanian countryside. Onboard amenities vary, but sleeping compartments are available on longer routes, and customs checks are carried out at border stations during the journey.

Once in the city, navigating Chisinau is both straightforward and economical, thanks to a robust network of public transportation options. The most iconic mode of transit is the trolleybus—an enduring symbol of Chisinau's urban landscape. These electric vehicles operate on over 20 routes across the city, offering a reliable, eco-friendly way to travel between neighborhoods, markets, parks, and landmarks. Trolleybuses run frequently from early morning until late evening, and fares are extremely affordable, making them a popular choice for locals and visitors alike. Passengers pay onboard by handing cash to the conductor, although mobile ticketing systems are gradually being introduced.

In addition to the trolleybus, a fleet of buses and minibuses—known locally as "rutieras"—covers routes that extend beyond the trolleybus grid, reaching suburbs and less accessible areas. While buses operate on set timetables, rutieras function more flexibly, often departing once full and stopping on request. Though faster and more direct, these minibuses can become crowded, especially during rush hours, and they may not always display clear route information. Still, they offer a unique glimpse into daily life in Chisinau, and those willing to engage with the experience will find them to be a practical and immersive form of transport.

Taxis and app-based ride services fill the gap between public transport and private mobility, with competitive prices and extensive coverage. In recent years, the use of mobile apps such as Yandex Go and Bolt has surged in popularity, especially among younger Moldovans and foreign visitors. These services allow users to choose from a range of vehicle types, track their ride in real-time, and pay via cash or card. They also offer the advantage of bypassing potential language barriers or price haggling. Traditional taxis are also available and can be hailed on the street or by phone, though it is advisable to choose reputable companies or hotel-recommended drivers to ensure a fair experience.

For travelers who prefer the freedom of a personal vehicle, renting a car in Chisinau is a viable and increasingly popular option. Several international and local car rental agencies operate at the airport and throughout the city, offering a broad selection of vehicles to suit different budgets and travel styles. From compact city cars to SUVs suitable for rural excursions, rentals can be arranged with ease, often including GPS navigation and insurance options. Most companies require drivers to be at least 21 years old with a valid license, and an International Driving Permit is recommended for those whose licenses are not printed in the Latin alphabet.

Driving in Chisinau and its surroundings is relatively straightforward, although it comes with nuances that visitors should be aware of. Road signs are typically in Romanian, and most follow international standards, but occasional Cyrillic signage may appear near Russian-speaking areas. The city's central districts can be congested during peak hours, and drivers should remain alert to pedestrians, cyclists, and occasional unpredictable maneuvers from local motorists. Parking is available throughout the city, both in public lots and on the street, but it may be limited in popular areas during busy times. Paid parking zones are clearly marked, and payment can often be made via mobile app or kiosk.

Venturing beyond Chisinau by car unlocks the beauty of Moldova's countryside, dotted with vineyards, monasteries, and hidden historical gems. Road conditions vary: while main highways are generally in good shape, secondary and rural roads may be less maintained and require cautious driving. Fuel is widely available and reasonably priced, with gas stations offering both traditional and self-service pumps. It's recommended to carry some cash for fuel and tolls, especially in more remote regions.

Overall, transportation to and within Chisinau provides flexibility, affordability, and a variety of experiences that suit all types of travelers. Whether arriving through the sleek corridors of the international airport, the timeworn charm of the railway station, or the open roads from neighboring countries, the journey into Moldova's capital sets the tone for a destination that is welcoming, accessible, and refreshingly authentic. The city's transport network reflects its gradual but steady modernization, offering visitors a seamless introduction to the rhythms of Chisinau life while ensuring the freedom to explore its many layers at a personal pace.

Chapter 4: Discovering Chisinau's Landmarks

The Grand National Assembly Square

The Nativity Cathedral

The Triumphal Arch

At the heart of Chisinau lies a trio of landmarks that together embody the city's identity, each one echoing Moldova's resilience, spiritual legacy, and historical transformation. These sites—The Grand National Assembly Square, the Nativity Cathedral, and the Triumphal Arch—are more than just architectural fixtures; they are symbols woven into the country's cultural and political tapestry, revered by Moldovans and admired by visitors who stand before them in search of meaning, memory, and beauty.

The Grand National Assembly Square is the geographical and symbolic epicenter of Chisinau. Sprawling and austere, it stands as an open arena of civic life and a stage for Moldova's most defining moments. This vast square is not merely a place of passage or leisure—it has been the scene of national celebrations, mass protests, cultural festivals, and solemn commemorations. Its name, drawn from the Great National Assembly that proclaimed Moldova's independence from the Soviet Union in 1991, reflects the enduring spirit of national pride that pulses through the capital. While its layout may appear plain at first glance, its magnitude and historical resonance give it a gravitas that commands reflection.

Flanked by key governmental and cultural buildings, the square invites visitors to understand Moldova not only through its past but also through its aspirations. The Parliament of the Republic of Moldova, with its imposing Soviet-modernist façade, anchors one side of the square, a tangible reminder of the country's political legacy and the ongoing journey of democracy. During national holidays like Independence Day and Language Day, the square comes alive with flags, traditional music, dancing, and public ceremonies that gather thousands from across the country. During quieter times, the wide expanse lends itself to contemplation, with people crossing by foot, pausing for photographs, or simply sitting on nearby benches to observe the steady rhythm of daily life.

Just steps away from the square, framed by rows of trees and pedestrian walkways, the Nativity Cathedral rises in graceful contrast. A masterpiece of neoclassical design, this whitewashed sanctuary with its domed bell tower and symmetrical colonnade is a beacon of spiritual calm in the city's bustling core. Originally built in 1836 under the direction of Russian architect Avraam Melnikov, the cathedral was commissioned during the Russian Empire's expansion into Bessarabia, reflecting both religious devotion and imperial ambition. Despite enduring decades of political upheaval, including destruction during World War II and Soviet suppression of religious practice, the cathedral has been lovingly restored and today stands as the principal church of the Moldovan Orthodox Church.

Crossing its threshold, visitors are often struck by the quiet solemnity within. The interior is a luminous space adorned with frescoes, golden iconostases, and the soft flicker of candles that echo the prayers of worshippers past and present. The cathedral's central dome soars above the nave, its celestial blue and gold ornamentation drawing the eyes heavenward. During Orthodox holidays—especially Easter and Christmas—the cathedral becomes the spiritual nucleus of Chisinau, with services that spill onto the surrounding square and draw crowds in a profound expression of faith and tradition.

Outside, the adjacent Cathedral Park offers a moment of tranquility, shaded by mature trees and populated by chess players, strolling families, and street musicians. This green space serves as a buffer from the city's hum, yet it is never isolated from the currents of daily life. It is not uncommon to find young couples lingering by the fountains or elderly residents quietly reading on benches, while tourists move between the cathedral and nearby landmarks. The park also contains several statues and memorials that honor literary and political figures, reinforcing the fusion of spiritual and civic memory found in this central quarter of Chisinau.

Dominating the park's southern edge, the Triumphal Arch provides yet another lens through which to view Moldova's complex narrative. Known locally as Arcul de Triumf, this 13-meter-high monument was constructed in 1840 to commemorate the victory of the Russian Empire over the Ottoman Empire in the Russo-Turkish War of 1828–1829. Though modest in scale compared to the grand triumphal arches of Western Europe, Chisinau's arch is a striking blend of classical symmetry and historical resonance. Made of pale stone and capped with a clock that continues to mark the hours over Stefan cel Mare Boulevard, it frames a line of sight toward the Government House on one side and the Nativity Cathedral on the other, creating an elegant urban axis that underscores the city's architectural coherence.

The Triumphal Arch is more than just a war monument—it has become an enduring emblem of

Chisinau itself. Its arches have witnessed generations of change: from imperial marches to Soviet parades, from independence rallies to peaceful protests. Today, it stands not as a celebration of conquest, but as a gateway into the soul of the city. Visitors passing beneath its vault often pause to take in the layered views it affords, or to photograph its clean lines against a backdrop of blue skies or golden sunsets.

Each of these landmarks offers its own dimension to the understanding of Chisinau. Together, they form a triad of civic, religious, and historical consciousness. The Grand National Assembly Square asserts the voice of the people and the strength of self-determination. The Nativity Cathedral offers sanctuary, continuity, and spiritual depth in a country that has often grappled with questions of identity. The Triumphal Arch binds past and present, framing both loss and legacy in enduring stone.

As a whole, the ensemble of these monuments speaks to a broader narrative of Moldova itself—a land shaped by empires but resilient in its independence, grounded in faith yet open to the world, modest in appearance but rich in substance. Walking this central corridor of Chisinau is not merely a sightseeing excursion; it is an intimate encounter with the country's historical heartbeat. The buildings do not shout for attention, yet they linger in memory long after the traveler has moved on, quietly telling their stories to those willing to listen.

Chapter 5: Immersing Yourself in Culture

The National Museum of History of Moldova

The National Museum of Ethnography and Natural History

The National Theatre of Opera and Ballet

Tucked within the cultural fabric of Chisinau are institutions that carry the voice of Moldova's history, identity, and creativity. To truly appreciate the city's soul, one must delve into its museums and theaters—places where artifacts speak, traditions breathe, and stories are rendered not only in words and objects, but also in movement, music, and art. Among the most compelling stops for those eager to immerse themselves in this cultural landscape are the National Museum of History of Moldova, the National Museum of Ethnography and Natural History, and the National Theatre of Opera and Ballet. Each offers a distinct portal into the Moldovan experience—past, present, and envisioned for the future.

The National Museum of History of Moldova stands as a cornerstone of national memory. Housed in a stately neoclassical building with roots stretching back to the early 20th century, this institution has long served as the keeper of the country's complex and often tumultuous historical record. Located on 31 August 1989 Street, the museum occupies what was once the building of a boys' gymnasium before being repurposed to preserve and interpret Moldova's past. Its architecture reflects a quiet dignity, with broad staircases, arched doorways, and airy galleries that lend a sense of reverence to the exhibits inside.

Stepping into the museum is like stepping into a time capsule that traces Moldova's development across centuries. The chronological journey begins in prehistory, with a fascinating collection of Paleolithic and Neolithic tools, pottery shards, and remnants of early dwellings. These archaeological treasures—many unearthed in sites such as Orheiul Vechi and the Prut and Dniester river valleys—are silent witnesses to human presence in the region for tens of thousands of years. Moving forward, the museum's classical and medieval exhibits showcase the evolution of Dacian tribes, Roman influence, and the principality of Moldavia's formation. Chainmail, ancient coins, religious relics, and intricate ceramics serve not only as artifacts but as emblems of Moldova's position at the crossroads of empires and cultures.

One of the most poignant sections of the museum is devoted to the modern era, particularly Moldova's time under Tsarist Russian control, its incorporation into the Soviet Union, and the eventual declaration of independence in 1991. Personal effects from political prisoners, propaganda posters, photographs from major uprisings, and documentary footage are woven into a powerful narrative of resistance, repression, and rebirth. A full-scale replica of Stephen the Great's sword, placed in one of the central halls, encapsulates the spirit of national pride that threads throughout the exhibitions.

Yet the museum does more than recount dates and dynasties. It also humanizes history through temporary exhibitions that reflect current social dialogues, as well as educational programs that connect youth with their heritage. For international visitors, many exhibits are labeled in multiple languages, and guided tours are readily available, making the experience both accessible and deeply enriching.

In contrast to the historical museum's linear approach to time, the National Museum of Ethnography and Natural History offers an immersive exploration of Moldova's traditions and biodiversity through a more sensory and thematic lens. Located in a striking building inspired by

Moorish architectural motifs, with ornate arched windows and geometric patterns, the museum is as much an aesthetic marvel as it is a cultural treasure. The interior, with its warm wood tones and thoughtfully curated displays, invites visitors to slow down and absorb the narratives embedded in the artifacts.

The ethnographic exhibits reveal the depth and richness of Moldovan rural life. Costumes embroidered with regional motifs, wooden household tools, farming implements, traditional musical instruments, and household ceramics are not presented as static objects but as carriers of story and identity. Each room reveals the interplay between ritual and routine—weddings, harvests, religious festivals, and seasonal customs all illustrated through life-size dioramas and multimedia presentations. The museum honors not just the objects themselves but the communities and values that created and sustained them over generations.

Perhaps the most unique aspect of the museum is its integration of natural history alongside ethnography. This dual focus reflects the intrinsic relationship between Moldovan people and their environment. Detailed taxidermy exhibits, geological samples, and botanical displays showcase the country's flora and fauna, including rare species native to the Codri forest and the steppe regions. A full skeleton of a Deinotherium gigantissimum—an extinct elephant-like creature that once roamed this land—takes center stage in the museum's main hall, both awe-inspiring and humbling in its prehistoric magnitude. The exhibit is a favorite among children and paleontology enthusiasts alike.

Walking through the galleries, visitors gain a profound sense of how Moldova's natural world has shaped its cultural expressions and how traditional knowledge was intimately tied to the rhythms of the land. Seasonal patterns dictated everything from agricultural cycles to clothing styles, and the museum beautifully portrays this interdependence. The museum is also a hub for conservation efforts and environmental education, reinforcing its role as a living institution dedicated not just to memory, but also to sustainable futures.

If the museums serve as windows into Moldova's past and ethnographic soul, the National Theatre of Opera and Ballet represents its dynamic present and artistic ambition. Situated in a grand building on Stefan cel Mare Boulevard, the theatre's stately white façade, adorned with classical columns and sculptural reliefs, announces a space of elegance and cultural prestige. Inside, the opulent red-and-gold auditorium, crowned with an ornate chandelier, provides a setting worthy of the world-class performances that grace its stage.

This is the beating heart of Moldova's high art, where voices soar, orchestras thunder, and stories unfold in the universal languages of music and movement. Founded in the mid-20th century during the Soviet period, the theater initially followed strict ideological lines, but quickly blossomed into a premier cultural institution with a growing repertoire and international acclaim.

Today, it continues to host a rich season of opera and ballet, ranging from classical masterpieces such as "La Traviata," "Swan Lake," and "Carmen," to Moldovan compositions and contemporary interpretations.

The theatre is renowned for the technical skill and emotional depth of its performers. Moldovan sopranos, tenors, and dancers have gained recognition far beyond the country's borders, often touring with prestigious companies in Europe and beyond. Yet the theatre's soul remains deeply local, with a loyal audience base and an artistic leadership committed to nurturing homegrown talent. Behind each performance is a disciplined troupe of artists, directors, set designers, and musicians who collaborate with passion and precision to deliver emotionally resonant shows.

What makes a night at the National Theatre of Opera and Ballet particularly memorable is its accessibility and intimacy. Unlike many European capitals where opera tickets can be prohibitively expensive or in short supply, Chisinau offers a chance to experience high culture in a welcoming and affordable setting. Performances are often subtitled, and the theater's warm acoustics and impeccable sightlines ensure that every seat offers an immersive experience. Whether attending a ballet on a crisp winter evening or a rousing opera during the summer season, visitors leave not only entertained, but moved by the artistic vitality of the city.

Together, these three institutions form a cultural triad that offers a deep, multidimensional understanding of

Chisinau. They bridge the ancient with the modern, the scientific with the spiritual, and the tangible with the emotional. In their galleries, halls, and stages, visitors encounter the voices of Moldova's ancestors, the craftsmanship of its villages, the marvels of its ecosystems, and the living pulse of its artistry. They are not just destinations, but journeys in themselves—rich in insight, vibrant in expression, and central to the story that this city so generously shares.

Chapter 6: Strolling Through Chisinau's Parks and Gardens

Stefan cel Mare Central Park

Valley of Roses Park (Valea Trandafirilor)

Botanical Garden

In the midst of Chisinau's urban rhythm, where Soviet-era architecture meets modern developments and historical monuments line the boulevards, the city's parks serve as sanctuaries of tranquility and natural splendor. These green spaces are more than places to relax; they are repositories of memory, venues for cultural life, and beloved gathering spots for generations of locals. Among them, three stand out for their central role in shaping Chisinau's identity and daily life: Stefan cel Mare Central Park, the Valley of Roses, and the sprawling Botanical Garden. Each offers a distinctive ambiance, inviting visitors into different layers of the city's ecological and social fabric.

Stefan cel Mare Central Park, located at the very heart of Chisinau, has been a cherished landmark for more than two centuries. Known informally as the "Park of the Lovers," it is not only the oldest park in the city but also one of its most symbolic. Originally established in 1818 during the Russian Imperial period and designed by architect Ozmidov, the park was envisioned as a formal European-style garden, laid out with a geometric precision that still lends it a sense of regal calm. Framed by ornate iron fencing and shaded by grand old linden trees, this park serves as both a green lung and a historical centerpiece.

Wandering through its elegant alleys, lined with benches and wrought-iron lampposts, is akin to stepping into a poetic tableau. A focal point of the park is the imposing statue of Stefan cel Mare, the 15th-century Moldovan ruler who defended the principality from Ottoman invasions and is revered as a national hero. Erected in 1928, the statue faces the Government House, standing as a symbolic protector of the city. The base of the monument is often surrounded by flowers, placed there by citizens during national holidays, commemorations, and even on quiet personal visits—underscoring the emotional attachment between the people and their past.

The park serves as a gathering place for locals and visitors alike, hosting everything from open-air concerts to peaceful solitary walks. On weekends, it's common to see artists sketching portraits, chess players engaged in animated duels, and couples strolling hand-in-hand under the sheltering trees. Seasonal blooms, particularly the tulips in spring and the golden leaves of autumn, transform the park into a living postcard. In winter, dusted with snow and twinkling with holiday lights, it assumes a serene, almost cinematic beauty. Beyond its aesthetics, Stefan cel Mare Central Park is embedded in the city's social life, bridging generations and offering a space for contemplation, conversation, and quiet joy.

While Stefan cel Mare Central Park represents the elegant, historical side of Chisinau's green spaces, the Valley of Roses, or Valea Trandafirilor, opens into a broader, more relaxed natural landscape that sprawls across the Botanica district. This is a favorite destination for families, joggers, and anyone seeking an escape from the denser city center. Encompassing over 80 hectares, the park's design centers around three interconnected lakes, which mirror the changing sky and offer cool breezes in the warmer months. The park's name stems from the profusion of rose bushes that bloom here during late spring and early summer, infusing the air with delicate fragrance and splashing the pathways with vibrant color.

Valea Trandafirilor was created during the Soviet period, in the 1960s, as part of a citywide initiative to integrate nature into urban planning. Its layout is more organic than that of Central Park, with winding trails, grassy meadows, and gently sloping hills that invite exploration. Paddle boats and small kayaks are available for rent on the lakes, while swans and ducks add a charming, pastoral touch. In the warmer months, this park transforms into a recreational hub, where families picnic beneath willow trees, children cycle along the paved paths, and vendors sell ice cream and roasted corn.

The park also features sports facilities, including tennis courts, volleyball courts, and outdoor gym equipment. Yet it never feels overcrowded; its sheer size ensures that there is always a quiet corner available for a peaceful afternoon. Outdoor cafes scattered around the lakes allow visitors to enjoy a coffee or a cold beer while taking in the view. The sound of birdsong is constant, and the sunsets, framed by leafy silhouettes, are unforgettable.

What sets the Valley of Roses apart is its ability to balance activity with calm. It serves as a public commons where both high energy and stillness are equally welcome. Local festivals and cultural events occasionally take place here, particularly during national holidays or seasonal celebrations. But more often, the park fulfills its quiet role in the everyday life of the city, offering an expansive green embrace to all who enter.

Further from the city center but no less significant is the Botanical Garden, officially known as the Chisinau Botanical Garden of the Academy of Sciences. This vast and richly varied site, occupying over 100 hectares in the southern part of the city, is a testament to Moldova's ecological diversity and scientific dedication. Established in 1950 and carefully developed over decades, the garden was designed not only for recreation but also for research, conservation, and education. It represents a harmonious blend of science and beauty, providing a refuge for rare species and a living classroom for botanists and nature enthusiasts.

The garden is divided into themed sections, each showcasing different plant ecosystems—ranging from alpine terrains and subtropical greenhouses to local steppe vegetation and aquatic habitats. Over 10,000 species of plants are cataloged and cultivated here, including ornamental shrubs, medicinal herbs, fruit trees, and exotic specimens from around the globe. In spring and early summer, the garden becomes a kaleidoscope of color, as rhododendrons, peonies, magnolias, and irises bloom in symphonic harmony.

One of the most enchanting areas of the Botanical Garden is the Japanese-style garden, complete with stone lanterns, wooden bridges, and meticulously pruned bonsai trees. It is a popular spot for wedding photography and quiet meditation. Another highlight is the vast greenhouse complex, which houses tropical plants including orchids, bromeliads, and towering banana palms that provide a warm, humid oasis even during the chilly Moldovan winters.

But the appeal of the Botanical Garden extends beyond its visual splendor. It functions as a research center for Moldova's environmental institutions and is actively involved in plant conservation and environmental education. Guided tours are available for those wishing to delve deeper into the scientific aspects of the garden, and during the academic year, students from Chisinau's universities frequently visit for lectures and field studies.

The garden also provides ample space for picnics, leisurely walks, and even cycling. Unlike the more structured Central Park or the recreational Valley of Roses, this space allows for a more exploratory experience. Birds nest in the thick canopies, butterflies flutter over flowerbeds, and the sound of rustling leaves is a near-constant companion. Whether you are a botanist, a photographer, or simply someone seeking peace, the Botanical Garden offers a kind of serenity that is rare in modern urban environments.

Taken together, these three parks illustrate the breadth and depth of Chisinau's relationship with nature. Each one reflects a different aspect of the city's personality—from the historical gravitas and symbolic importance of Stefan cel Mare Central Park, to the recreational openness of Valea Trandafirilor, and the scientific curiosity and tranquility of the Botanical Garden. More than just beautiful green spaces, they are living components of the city's daily rhythm, shaped by the people who frequent them and the natural world they protect and display. A walk through any of these places is not just a leisure activity—it is a chance to understand the city on a deeper, more personal level.

Chapter 7: Uncovering Hidden Gems

Exploring the Old Town Area

Discovering Local Markets

Architectural Highlights Beyond the Center

Tucked into the gentle hills and winding streets of Chisinau is a side of the city often overlooked by those who stick to the grand boulevards and polished public squares. The Old Town area, though partially lost to war, time, and the sweeping changes of Soviet urban planning, still whispers stories of the past through cobbled alleys, crumbling façades, and centuries-old churches that remain standing as guardians of heritage. While Chisinau may not boast a preserved old quarter like Prague or Krakow, those who venture through its oldest districts discover a uniquely Moldovan narrative — one shaped by resilience, subtle elegance, and a multicultural mosaic that continues to color the city's present.

The Old Town is not a single, clearly demarcated zone, but rather a collection of historic streets and buildings, mostly located near the Rășcani and Centru sectors. Here, travelers can feel a tangible difference in rhythm — life moves slower, the architecture grows more eclectic, and a strong sense of identity lingers in the uneven stone pavements and ornate gates. The surviving pre-Soviet architecture mixes neoclassical and baroque influences with local vernacular styles. Many buildings have weathered façades, adorned with intricate cornices, wrought-iron balconies, and wooden shutters, bearing the wear of generations but retaining their beauty.

Among the notable structures is the Măzărache Church, considered the oldest in the city, built in the 18th century on the ruins of a former fortress. Its modest stone construction and classic Moldavian silhouette reflect the architectural restraint of a time when churches were built to endure, not impress. Just steps away, the Armenian Church of Chisinau, though often closed to the public, stands as a quiet reminder of the ethnic diversity that once flourished in the city. Jewish synagogues, some still functioning, others repurposed or fading into the urban fabric, speak to a rich past that saw Chisinau as a multicultural crossroad.

Walking through these streets, visitors can also spot details that survived Soviet reconstruction efforts — ornate door frames, cast-iron signage in faded Romanian Cyrillic, and hidden courtyards shaded by grapevines. These places are best discovered on foot, preferably without a strict itinerary, as the charm of the Old Town lies in its unexpected corners and lived-in authenticity. Time-worn residential houses sit beside modest artisan workshops and cafes with mismatched furniture and strong black coffee. Locals often sit outside, chatting in Romanian or Russian, creating a soundtrack of multilingual hum that reflects the city's complex heritage.

Woven into this historical landscape is another beating heart of the city — its vibrant local markets. These are not simply places to shop but are immersive cultural experiences that offer a raw and flavorful introduction to Moldovan life. The most famous is Piata Centrala, Chisinau's central market, located just southeast of the city center. Stretching across several blocks, it is a sprawling and energetic expanse where fresh produce, household goods, flowers, clothes, cheeses, meats, and spices are sold side by side in a joyous sort of chaos. The market has been operating in one form or another since the 19th century, and today it draws a steady stream of both residents and visitors.

At first glance, Piata Centrala might seem overwhelming, with vendors calling out prices, carts squeaking down narrow paths, and customers haggling under tarpaulin-covered stalls. But this controlled disorder hides remarkable efficiency and hospitality. It is a place where the seasons dictate what is on display — from sweet cherries and wild strawberries in June to mountains of cabbages and pumpkins in autumn. Moldovan dairy products, especially brânză (a soft white cheese), are a staple, often sold directly by farmers from nearby villages. The same goes for honey, wine, and homemade preserves, with many sellers offering tastes before you buy.

In addition to fresh goods, the market is an excellent spot to pick up local handicrafts, such as handwoven textiles, traditional ceramics, and carved wooden kitchenware. On the periphery of the main stalls are makeshift booths that appear almost organically — men selling tools, old Soviet badges, and even vintage cameras, while women knit woolen socks or sell jars of pickled vegetables. It's a space where commerce meets conversation, and where even a brief exchange with a vendor can reveal insights into Moldovan hospitality, humor, and pride.

Not far from Piata Centrala, one can find other markets and bazaars that cater more specifically to niche needs or neighborhoods, including the flower market on Bucuresti Street and the art market near Stefan cel Mare Park. The latter is a favorite for those looking for oil paintings, folk costumes, or Soviet memorabilia. These open-air settings offer not only shopping opportunities but a chance to connect directly with local artisans and understand the city's aesthetics and values through their work.

As one steps outside the central grid of Chisinau, new architectural layers begin to emerge — grandiose, understated, experimental, and occasionally contradictory. The city's architectural story is complex, shaped by multiple empires, ideological shifts, and socioeconomic transformations. Beyond the center, residential neighborhoods and lesser-known districts reveal architectural highlights that deserve exploration for their cultural significance and visual intrigue.

The 20th century left the strongest imprint on Chisinau's skyline, with Soviet-era constructions dominating large portions of the urban landscape. While some of these buildings are utilitarian and austere, others reflect a form of monumental modernism that has aged into architectural curiosity. The Circus building, with its flying saucer-like design and brutalist flair, is a haunting relic of Moldova's Soviet past, standing as both an icon and a cautionary tale of ambitious public projects. Though no longer regularly in use, it remains a powerful symbol and a striking photo opportunity.

In the Telecentru district, one can find curious examples of Soviet-era apartment blocks interspersed with more contemporary villas and embassies. This juxtaposition is emblematic of Chisinau's post-independence architectural evolution, as the city seeks to reconcile its history with new economic and cultural aspirations. The skyline is dotted with spires from Orthodox churches, glass-fronted office towers, and aging gray concrete — a reflection of Moldova's transitions and aspirations.

One of the more interesting architectural developments lies in the adaptive reuse of older buildings. Former factories, bathhouses, and even schools are being transformed into cafes, co-working spaces, and galleries, particularly in areas undergoing revitalization efforts. The emergence of places like the ARTICO building and the adjacent Creative Industries Center reveals how local architects and designers are engaging with historical forms while injecting new energy and function into outdated structures.

Among the hidden gems is the Chișinău Water Tower, now functioning as part of the city's historical museum complex. Its red brick and rounded form stand in sharp contrast to the more prevalent Soviet styles and highlight the city's early 20th-century aspirations toward Western European aesthetics. Walking through these areas, attentive visitors may also spot former merchant homes, their once-opulent façades now softened by ivy or painted in pastel colors. These buildings tell stories of a pre-revolutionary Chisinau when the city was a trading hub between empires, enriched by its Jewish, Armenian, Russian, and Romanian communities.

Each structure, street, and market stall encountered in these explorations contributes to a deeper understanding of Chisinau. This is not a city that reveals all its charms at once. It asks for curiosity, rewards patience, and delivers authenticity. Whether navigating the nuanced history of its Old Town, savoring the abundance of its markets, or admiring the odd beauty of its architectural contrasts, visitors are invited not just to see, but to feel the heartbeat of a place that continues to evolve while holding firmly to its roots.

Chapter 8: Venturing into Moldova's Wine Country

Visiting Cricova Winery

Exploring Milestii Mici Winery

Other Notable Wine Tours

Nestled within the rolling hills just beyond Chisinau lies one of Moldova's most celebrated treasures — its wine country, an enchanting landscape of vineyards, limestone tunnels, and centuries-old winemaking traditions. For travelers eager to explore Moldova's rich viticultural heritage, a journey into this world is not simply a tasting experience, but a full immersion into the country's identity. Moldovan wine is more than a product; it is a reflection of resilience, artistry, and a deep connection to the land. Among the crown jewels of this heritage are two globally renowned wineries: Cricova and Milestii Mici. Each offers a unique glimpse into the alchemy of winemaking and provides experiences that engage the senses while revealing the enduring craftsmanship behind every bottle.

Just 15 kilometers north of Chisinau, Cricova Winery is a subterranean wonder and a must-visit for anyone curious about Moldova's wine legacy. Often referred to as a "wine city," Cricova's labyrinthine cellars stretch over 120 kilometers underground, transforming a vast limestone mine into a kingdom of barrels, bottles, and fermentation halls. Entering the tunnels is like stepping into a secret world — a realm where temperature and humidity are precisely controlled to nurture thousands of wines as they rest in patient silence. The tunnels are so expansive that visitors tour them by electric vehicle, driving past streets humorously named after grape varieties like Cabernet, Pinot, and Feteasca.

Founded in 1952 during the Soviet era, Cricova quickly gained a reputation as a prestigious producer, supplying wines to Soviet leaders and foreign dignitaries. Today, it balances tradition with innovation, crafting wines that have won international accolades while maintaining time-honored methods of production. One of Cricova's unique features is its sparkling wine production, developed using the classic French "Méthode Champenoise." This meticulous process involves secondary fermentation in the bottle, a technique that requires patience and precision. The result is a refined collection of sparkling wines with delicate bubbles and a rich, creamy texture.

Visitors to Cricova can choose from several guided tours that typically include a journey through the cellars, a walk through the museum halls filled with vintage equipment and historical documents, and a glimpse of the "National Collection," a vault that houses rare and collectible wines. One of the most fascinating bottles here is said to belong to Hermann Göring, seized by the Soviets during World War II and now kept as a historical artifact. The tour often concludes in one of Cricova's atmospheric tasting halls, each uniquely themed and elaborately decorated — from medieval-style banqueting rooms to elegant marble salons. Wine tastings are paired with local cheeses, meats, and breads, offering a sensory connection to Moldovan cuisine and terroir.

Further south, about 18 kilometers from Chisinau, lies another of Moldova's vinous marvels: Milestii Mici Winery. Recognized by the Guinness Book of World Records as housing the largest wine collection in the world, Milestii Mici's cellars extend for over 200 kilometers, although about 55 kilometers are actively used for storage and tours. Like Cricova, these cellars were originally limestone quarries, transformed into a massive underground storage facility where the natural environment — constant temperature and humidity — creates the ideal conditions for aging wine.

Milestii Mici is a more rustic and less polished experience compared to Cricova's theatrical charm, but what it lacks in showmanship it makes up for in sheer scale and authenticity. The "Golden Collection," stored within the depths of these tunnels, includes nearly two million bottles of wine — some aging for decades. The wines of Milestii Mici are known for their rich body, deep color, and robust character, with particular attention paid to reds such as Merlot, Cabernet Sauvignon, and native Moldovan varietals like Rara Neagra. Their dry reds, matured in oak barrels and glass bottles for extended periods, are especially notable for their intensity and smooth tannins.

The tour at Milestii Mici typically begins with a descent into the cavernous corridors, winding through streets lined with bottle after bottle, some labeled by decade and others resting quietly without identification, waiting for their time to shine. Many of the guides here are long-time employees with deep knowledge of the winery's history and techniques, and their narratives are filled with personal anecdotes and folklore. After the tour, guests are invited to one of the underground tasting rooms, decorated in traditional Moldovan style with carved wood, handwoven textiles, and warm, rustic touches. The tastings include a selection of house wines accompanied by local fare — smoked meats, pickled vegetables, and hearty bread — all served with genuine Moldovan hospitality.

Beyond Cricova and Milestii Mici, Moldova's wine country is dotted with smaller, boutique wineries that offer equally rich, if more intimate, experiences. Purcari Winery, located in the Stefan Voda region, about two hours from Chisinau, is among the most prestigious of these. Founded in 1827, it has a long-standing tradition of excellence, with its wines historically favored by European royalty, including Queen Victoria. The estate combines history, modern winemaking, and luxury accommodation, making it a complete retreat for wine enthusiasts. Its Negru de Purcari blend — a mix of Cabernet Sauvignon, Rara Neagra, and Saperavi — is internationally celebrated and encapsulates the powerful yet elegant profile of Moldovan reds.

Et Cetera, a family-owned winery in the southern region of the country, offers a more relaxed and contemporary wine tourism experience. The owners, the Luchianov family, focus on small-batch production with a dedication to quality and sustainability. Guests are welcomed like friends, and the tours often feel more like a visit to a countryside home than a commercial facility. Their wines — particularly the white blends and rose — are light, refreshing, and well-suited to Moldova's warm climate. The estate includes a restaurant and guesthouse, inviting travelers to stay overnight and enjoy the peaceful rhythms of rural Moldovan life.

Chateau Vartely, near the town of Orhei, is another name that has gained recognition for both its wine and its commitment to tourism. The estate offers structured tastings, cellar tours, and overnight accommodations in well-appointed villas. With panoramic views of surrounding vineyards and a focus on both international and indigenous varietals, Chateau Vartely provides a well-rounded experience that appeals to novices and connoisseurs alike.

Each of these wine destinations contributes to a broader narrative — one that reveals Moldova not just as a wine producer, but as a wine culture. This is a place where vines are not merely cultivated but revered, where the rhythm of village life is marked by the changing seasons of the vineyard, and where wine is a medium through which stories are told, traditions passed down, and community is celebrated. Whether in the grand halls of Cricova, the endless corridors of Milestii Mici, or the sun-drenched patios of boutique estates, visitors discover more than just wine — they discover a deeply rooted sense of place.

The road to Moldova's wine cellars is paved with history, flavor, and a quiet passion that thrives beyond the gaze of mass tourism. For those willing to explore it, this journey becomes a celebration of authenticity, where every glass poured invites a deeper understanding of the land, its people, and the remarkable resilience that defines Moldova's spirit.

Chapter 9: Day Trips to Historical Sites

Orheiul Vechi Archaeological Complex

Tipova Monastery

Soroca Fortress

High on the limestone cliffs above the Răut River lies one of Moldova's most remarkable and evocative destinations: the Orheiul Vechi Archaeological Complex. This expansive cultural landscape, situated about an hour's drive northeast of the capital, is both a testament to Moldova's layered history and a deeply spiritual place that still breathes with life. From the moment one arrives, the land tells a story — of ancient civilizations, medieval monks, and the unbroken continuity of Moldovan rural tradition. Its dramatic topography, where rocky outcrops tower above meandering waters and green meadows, only adds to its sense of timeless wonder.

Orheiul Vechi is not a single monument, but a collection of ruins, natural formations, and inhabited villages that span several millennia of history. Archaeological excavations have revealed settlements dating back to the Dacians, as well as remnants from the Golden Horde, the Moldavian Principality, and even Roman incursions. One of the most striking aspects of the site is its troglodyte monastery, carved directly into the limestone rock. These monastic caves, believed to have been excavated by Orthodox monks around the 13th century, served as both places of worship and sanctuary during times of invasion. Today, the monastery is still active, and visitors may find a solitary monk in prayer, candles flickering in the dim silence of the stone-hewn chapel.

Above the caves stands a small white church with a bell tower, built in the early 20th century. From here, the view is panoramic — a sweep of the valley below that captures the rustic charm of the villages, the serpentine river, and the vast Moldovan steppe. Pilgrims and tourists alike climb the steps to this church, drawn not only by its religious significance but also by the magnetic tranquility that surrounds it. The entire complex feels less like a museum and more like a living, breathing site of heritage, where ancient rituals and everyday life continue to coexist.

The surrounding villages, such as Butuceni and Trebujeni, preserve traditional Moldovan life with remarkable authenticity. Stone cottages with thatched roofs, narrow lanes, and blooming gardens create an atmosphere untouched by the rush of modern development. Many families here open their homes to visitors, offering not only accommodation but also meals made from homegrown produce and regional recipes. A stay in Butuceni is an opportunity to immerse oneself in the rhythms of pastoral life — to wake to the crowing of roosters, taste freshly baked bread from clay ovens, and engage in heartfelt conversation over homemade wine.

Farther afield, perched above the rocky cliffs along the Dniester River, lies the hauntingly beautiful Tipova Monastery. Unlike the compact complex at Orheiul Vechi, Tipova stretches along a wild and remote gorge, with its monastic cells and chapels cut into the rugged cliffside over a distance of several hundred meters. The sense of isolation here is profound, enhanced by the

62

sound of rushing water from nearby waterfalls and the calls of birds that nest in the stone crevices. The journey to Tipova is part of the experience — a winding road through forests and villages that culminates in a descent into the dramatic canyon.

According to tradition, Tipova Monastery dates back to the 11th century and was expanded over the centuries by monastic communities seeking refuge and contemplation. Local legends suggest that Stephen the Great, Moldova's national hero, visited Tipova and that his wife may have been buried here, though historical evidence is inconclusive. What is certain, however, is the monastery's enduring spiritual aura. The complex includes several small chapels, modest cells for monks, and larger communal spaces, all carved from the rock with astounding craftsmanship. The cliffside paths connecting the structures are narrow and uneven, offering a taste of the hardship and devotion that characterized monastic life.

Visitors often describe Tipova as one of the most powerful places they encounter in Moldova. There is a primal beauty in the way the stone walls absorb the sunlight, in the interplay of moss, shadow, and silence. The experience is contemplative, even humbling — a retreat into nature and spirit where time seems suspended. In the spring and autumn, when wildflowers bloom or golden leaves fall like confetti into the gorge, the site is particularly enchanting. Nearby, the Tipova waterfall — one of Moldova's highest — adds an element of natural spectacle, tumbling over rocks with a fierce energy that contrasts with the stillness of the monastery.

To the north, close to the Ukrainian border, stands another of Moldova's historical landmarks: Soroca Fortress. Situated on the banks of the Dniester River, this perfectly circular stone fortress has stood for centuries as a symbol of Moldova's resistance and architectural prowess. Its location, once a strategic military outpost on the frontier of the medieval Moldavian Principality, allowed it to guard the river crossing and repel invaders. Built in its current form in the 16th century by Stephen the Great's son, Petru Rareș, the fortress replaced a former wooden stronghold and became one of the most advanced defensive constructions of its time.

What sets Soroca Fortress apart is its symmetry and precision. The circular plan, fortified by five bastions arranged at equal intervals, is an example of Renaissance military design adapted to local conditions. The thick stone walls and elevated towers offered protection against both gunpowder weapons and siege tactics. As one walks through the fortress gates and into the central courtyard, it's easy to imagine the soldiers, horses, and blacksmiths that once animated this place during times of war and peace.

In recent years, Soroca Fortress has undergone substantial restoration, preserving its original layout while enhancing accessibility for visitors. The interior now includes interpretive displays on the history of the region, weapons used in its defense, and the architectural innovations that made the fortress a marvel of its era. Climbing the towers provides sweeping views of the Dniester and the green hills beyond — a vista that has remained largely unchanged for generations. On a clear day, one can see into Ukraine, a reminder of the fortress's strategic role at the edge of Moldova's cultural landscape.

The town of Soroca itself is worth exploring. Known as Moldova's "Roma capital," it is home to a vibrant Romani community with its own unique traditions and architectural styles. One of the most unusual sights here is the so-called "Roma Hill," where large and ornate houses — often resembling palaces — reflect the aspirations and cultural identity of the Roma elite. These colorful homes, adorned with columns, domes, and eclectic detailing, stand in stark contrast to the medieval austerity of the fortress, offering a different but equally compelling narrative of Moldova's social fabric.

Taken together, these three destinations — Orheiul Vechi, Tipova Monastery, and Soroca Fortress — offer a multidimensional journey through Moldova's spiritual, historical, and cultural terrain. They reveal the endurance of ancient beliefs, the ingenuity of defensive architecture, and the quiet dignity of rural life. To visit them is to move beyond the urban rhythm of the capital and into the soul of the country, where history is etched into rock, ritual is preserved in silence, and every landscape tells a story that bridges centuries.

Chapter 10: Exploring Nature and Outdoors

Condrita Monastery and Surroundings

Capriana Monastery and Forests

Hiking and Nature Trails Near Chisinau

Tucked away in the hilly forests that stretch west of Chisinau, Condrița Monastery emerges like a hidden sanctuary, quietly nestled among centuries-old trees and whispering winds. Though less frequently visited than its more famous counterparts, this Orthodox monastic complex holds an atmosphere of solemn peace, making it a rewarding retreat for those seeking spiritual reflection or a deeper connection with Moldova's religious and cultural heritage. Founded in the 18th century under the patronage of Moldavian princes, the monastery has long served as a place of monastic devotion and regional pilgrimage, offering a serene escape into a world governed by timeless ritual and natural tranquility.

As the road winds into the village of Condrița, the forest seems to close in gently, embracing the monastery in a curtain of green. The complex reveals itself in parts—first the high stone walls, then the domes and crosses of the church buildings peeking through the trees. Unlike larger, more touristic religious sites, Condrița retains a humble and authentic atmosphere. The main church, with its classic Orthodox architecture and weather-worn frescoes, invites visitors to step inside not only as observers but as guests in a living space of prayer. Monks still inhabit the site, tending to the gardens, restoring icons, and maintaining centuries-old traditions that bind faith to everyday life.

Surrounding the monastery, the natural setting plays an equal role in the experience. The thick woods are a symphony of birdsong and rustling leaves, offering ideal conditions for quiet contemplation or leisurely exploration. The nearby hills and forested trails form a microcosm of Moldova's rural charm—untouched, genuine, and deeply nourishing to the soul. In spring and autumn, when wildflowers blanket the forest floor or when golden foliage lines the paths, the landscape around Condrița becomes a painter's palette, bursting with color and soft light.

Not far from Condrița lies another emblem of Moldova's ecclesiastical heritage: the Capriana Monastery, one of the oldest and most revered religious sites in the country. Situated within the Codrii Forest, Moldova's largest stretch of ancient woodland, Capriana holds an enduring place in the national consciousness, not only as a sacred site but as a cornerstone of Moldovan identity. Founded in the 15th century, the monastery rose to prominence during the reign of Stephen the Great, who is believed to have been a key patron. Over the centuries, it became a cultural beacon—home to Moldova's first printing press, a vibrant center for manuscript copying, and a gathering place for theologians, writers, and scholars.

The monastery's architectural ensemble is a harmonious blend of structures built over different historical periods, including the Church of the Dormition, which dates to the early 20th century, and older chapels and residential buildings that carry the aesthetic of earlier centuries. The main church, with its ornate iconostasis and richly adorned walls, creates an immediate sense of spiritual gravitas. Pilgrims often come here during religious festivals, especially on major Orthodox feast days, when the courtyard fills with incense, choral singing, and the flow of candle-bearing worshippers. Despite its historical stature, the monastery does not feel overly grandiose. Instead, it conveys a feeling of gentle reverence, grounded in the peaceful rhythms of nature that surround it.

The forests of Capriana stretch in every direction—miles of old-growth oak, linden, and hornbeam trees form a living canopy over the rolling hills. The region is a paradise for nature lovers and offers a number of hiking paths that wind through glades, streambeds, and sun-dappled clearings. Some of these trails are part of designated eco-tourism routes, complete with signage and resting areas, while others follow traditional footpaths once used by shepherds and villagers. A walk through these woods can be meditative or invigorating, depending on the pace and direction. One might encounter deer moving silently through the underbrush or stumble upon the ruins of forgotten chapels blanketed in moss.

For those who seek a more structured outdoor adventure, the wider area around Chisinau provides a growing network of hiking and nature trails designed to showcase Moldova's ecological and cultural diversity. The country's compact size works in favor of day trippers, with most trails reachable within an hour or two of the capital. One particularly popular route follows the forested ridges west of Capriana, passing through the Codrii Nature Reserve—a protected area home to some of the rarest flora and fauna in Moldova. With elevation changes, panoramic viewpoints, and dense biodiversity, this trail offers a moderate challenge and the kind of solitude rarely found in more crowded hiking destinations across Europe.

Other nature trails branch off from villages near the Lapusna and Lozova regions, winding past small lakes, sunflower fields, and forest chapels that serve as reminders of Moldova's spiritual roots. These routes often lead to high ridges offering sweeping views of the surrounding countryside—rolling farmland dotted with haystacks, orchards, and the occasional horse-drawn cart moving along a dirt road. Each vista tells a story of continuity and resilience, a landscape unchanged in many ways since the time of Moldova's earliest chroniclers.

Though not always well-marked or mapped, these trails provide opportunities for authentic exploration, particularly for those who prefer paths less traveled. Local guides and community-based tourism initiatives have become increasingly important in helping visitors navigate the routes while preserving the ecological balance of the area. In some villages, families offer food and lodging to hikers, creating a network of rural hospitality that enhances the outdoor experience. Here, the warmth of a shared meal, the taste of homemade cheese and wine, or the simplicity of a quiet night in a village home can become just as memorable as the hike itself.

Seasonality plays a significant role in shaping the hiking experience. Spring brings a rush of life, with wildflowers carpeting the forest floor and birds returning to nest in the trees. Summer offers long days and rich green canopies, while autumn transforms the landscape into a mosaic of amber, crimson, and ochre. Even winter, though cold and at times impassable due to snow, has its charm—frost-covered branches, the crunch of boots on frozen ground, and the solitude of a forest in hibernation.

Together, the monasteries of Condrița and Capriana and the surrounding nature trails form an interconnected mosaic of spirituality, history, and ecology. They offer not only physical journeys into Moldova's heartland but also emotional and philosophical encounters with a way of life rooted in balance—between man and nature, faith and reason, past and present. These sites are not merely destinations, but invitations to slow down, breathe deeply, and rediscover the quiet majesty of places shaped more by centuries of reverence than by the demands of modern tourism.

In these forests and sacred spaces, time seems to stretch and soften. One begins to walk not just through Moldova, but with it—along its paths, into its chapels, and through its living silence. The journey lingers, long after the dust is shaken from boots and the roads lead back to the city.

Chapter 11: Accommodation Options in Chisinau

Hotels and Guesthouses

Apartment Rentals

Budget-Friendly Choices

In Chisinau, accommodation is more than just a place to sleep; it offers a window into the evolving identity of Moldova's capital, shaped by history, post-Soviet resilience, and a steadily growing tourism sector. Whether travelers seek modern luxury, quiet guesthouse charm, long-term comfort, or affordable efficiency, the city provides a spectrum of lodging that caters to diverse needs and styles.

The city's hotels range from internationally recognized establishments to locally owned boutique spaces, each with its own distinct ambiance. At the top end of the spectrum, international chains like Radisson Blu and Bristol Central have established a foothold, offering high-end experiences with amenities that meet or exceed European standards. These hotels typically feature spacious rooms, well-equipped business centers, upscale dining, and wellness areas complete with saunas, fitness centers, and spa services. Located in the heart of Chisinau or near major government buildings, they attract diplomats, business travelers, and those looking to indulge in comfort while remaining close to the city's cultural landmarks and nightlife.

However, Chisinau's character is often better captured in its locally run boutique hotels and guesthouses, which blend tradition and hospitality with a personal touch. These smaller lodgings tend to be set in refurbished historic buildings or post-war architecture, offering a more intimate atmosphere. Many are family-operated, and their hosts are quick to offer local insights, arrange transportation, or recommend restaurants that aren't yet on the mainstream tourist map. Some have lush courtyard gardens, homemade breakfast options, or vintage Moldovan decor that immerses visitors in a sense of place. Unlike more standardized hotel offerings, these guesthouses reflect the warm and understated charm that Moldova is increasingly known for.

Away from the central core, neighborhoods like Botanica and Riscani present mid-range hotel options that balance affordability with convenience. These areas are ideal for travelers seeking a quieter stay without sacrificing easy access to parks, museums, and public transport. Some hotels in these districts occupy former Soviet buildings that have been tastefully modernized, blending old-world sturdiness with sleek interiors, high-speed internet, and contemporary furnishings. Their appeal lies not just in price, but in their proximity to authentic Chisinau life—markets bustling with locals, unpretentious eateries, and tree-lined streets that feel a world away from the more polished downtown area.

For those staying longer or simply preferring more independence, apartment rentals provide another excellent option. Over the past decade, platforms such as Airbnb and local rental services have grown rapidly in Chisinau, making it easy to find a wide array of apartments in every corner of the city. From modern studios in high-rise buildings to spacious, multi-room flats with classic Eastern European design, the variety is considerable. Apartment stays often appeal to digital nomads, small families, and solo travelers who enjoy the freedom of cooking their own meals or maintaining a flexible schedule. Kitchens are typically equipped with essentials, and most rentals include Wi-Fi, laundry facilities, and sometimes balconies with expansive views over the city's tree canopies and domed churches.

The advantage of apartment rentals lies not only in privacy and space but in the opportunity to live like a local. Neighborhood bakeries become morning rituals, nearby grocers serve as introductions to Moldovan ingredients, and the rhythm of daily life becomes a backdrop to the travel experience. It's also a more budget-friendly solution for groups or families, offering multiple rooms at a fraction of the cost of hotel suites.

For travelers conscious of cost, Chisinau is a welcoming destination. Budget-friendly choices are widely available and can be surprisingly comfortable, clean, and centrally located. Hostels have gained traction, especially among younger travelers, with several well-rated options offering dorm beds and private rooms at very accessible rates. These hostels are typically located near key attractions and often provide communal kitchens, social areas, and sometimes organized city tours or language exchange nights. They serve as excellent hubs for meeting fellow travelers and getting tips from experienced staff on how to explore Chisinau on a modest budget.

Beyond hostels, budget hotels and pension-style lodgings cater to those looking for private rooms at minimal cost. While amenities may be more basic—think smaller rooms, simpler furnishings, or shared bathrooms—the hospitality often compensates. Staff at such places tend to go the extra mile, arranging early check-ins, calling taxis, or offering complimentary tea and coffee. It's common to find establishments that have been running for decades, each with its own quirks, stories, and loyal clientele.

An additional feature of Chisinau's budget accommodation scene is its low season pricing flexibility. During off-peak months, many hotels and apartment owners lower their rates, creating opportunities for extended stays without stretching the wallet. This flexibility is particularly attractive for remote workers or slow travelers who value affordability without compromising on comfort or location.

It's worth noting that Moldova's overall cost of living is among the lowest in Europe, and this affordability extends across the hospitality industry. Even mid-range hotels often offer nightly rates that are significantly below what one might expect in comparable European capitals. For this reason, travelers may find themselves able to "upgrade" to more luxurious options while still staying within a modest budget. Upscale hotels and apartments that include breakfast, airport transfers, and concierge services become realistic choices for a wide range of visitors.

Safety and convenience are also central to the accommodation experience in Chisinau. Most hotel staff speak at least conversational English, and signs in accommodations tend to be available in both Romanian and English. Booking through established platforms, checking recent reviews, and confirming amenities in advance helps ensure a smooth stay. Payment methods are flexible, with most hotels and rentals accepting credit cards, while smaller guesthouses and hostels may prefer cash payments in Moldovan lei.

Location is an important factor when selecting where to stay. The city center remains the most convenient base for first-time visitors, offering walkable access to major sights like the Cathedral Park, the Triumphal Arch, and a vibrant stretch of restaurants and cafes along Stefan cel Mare Boulevard. However, staying slightly outside the center can offer a more peaceful experience without significantly reducing accessibility. Public transport, including minibuses and trolleybuses, makes getting around affordable and straightforward, even from peripheral neighborhoods.

The diversity of lodging in Chisinau reflects the city's gradual yet thoughtful modernization. Each type of accommodation—be it a historic guesthouse, a sleek apartment, a cheerful hostel, or a five-star hotel—presents a different angle on the capital's culture and its people. Where one stays can shape the entire narrative of a visit, offering more than just rest, but genuine immersion into a city that is quietly coming into its own. Whether travelers come for a weekend or a month, whether their budget is generous or limited, there is a space in Chisinau that feels like home, a place where comfort and authenticity coexist in harmony.

Chapter 12: Dining and Nightlife

Traditional Moldovan Cuisine

International Dining Options

Bars, Pubs, and Clubs

Chisinau's culinary landscape is a vibrant mosaic that reflects the city's multi-ethnic identity, rural roots, and its growing embrace of global flavors. At its heart lies traditional Moldovan cuisine, a hearty and soulful expression of the country's agrarian heritage. Rooted in peasant traditions and influenced by neighboring cultures, Moldovan food offers a rich narrative of history, resilience, and community, best experienced through its timeless dishes, communal eating, and locally sourced ingredients.

A culinary journey in Chisinau often begins with *mămăligă*, a staple cornmeal porridge similar to polenta, often served with sour cream, salty sheep cheese, and sometimes a generous ladle of pork stew or mushroom sauce. This dish, simple yet deeply satisfying, is symbolic of Moldovan hospitality—nourishing, rustic, and always best enjoyed with company. Another classic is *sarmale*, small parcels of cabbage or grape leaves wrapped around a filling of rice and minced meat, slow-cooked in a tangy tomato broth. The patience and precision involved in preparing sarmale echo the country's values of craftsmanship and familial tradition.

Soups are foundational to the Moldovan table, especially *zeamă*, a light chicken broth enriched with homemade noodles, garden vegetables, and flavored with a fermented wheat bran called *borș*. Often served with a side of fresh bread and hot peppers, zeamă is considered both comfort food and a ceremonial dish, appearing at family gatherings and festive occasions. Heavier fare includes grilled meats such as *mici*—spiced minced meat rolls, typically served with mustard and a cold beer. Roasted duck, pork ribs, and rabbit stew also appear on many menus, often accompanied by pickled vegetables and seasonal salads.

Desserts reflect the rural abundance of fruits and nuts, with pies filled with sour cherries or apples, and pastries like *plăcintă*, which can be savory or sweet. Walnut-stuffed crepes drizzled with honey and homemade jams are common, especially in colder months. Moldova's wines, both white and red, naturally accompany meals. The country's winemaking tradition spans thousands of years, and local wines are not just pairings—they are part of the meal's soul. Dry whites from the central Codru region or full-bodied reds from the south are served proudly in nearly every restaurant, with some establishments offering house wines produced by small, family-run vineyards.

Many of the best places to taste traditional Moldovan food in Chisinau are restaurants that pay homage to rustic aesthetics, with interiors styled after village homes—wooden beams, embroidered linens, clay pots, and even live folk music on certain evenings. These venues blend theater and authenticity, offering more than just a meal—they offer a cultural performance in which diners are participants in a centuries-old story.

Beyond tradition, Chisinau has increasingly positioned itself as a modern European city with a growing international culinary scene. As the capital becomes more cosmopolitan, so too does its food. Over the past decade, a wave of new restaurants, bistros, and cafes has emerged, each bringing global cuisines into the local context. Italian trattorias, French patisseries, Japanese sushi bars, and Middle Eastern eateries are now found throughout the city, particularly in central districts like Buiucani and Centru.

Italian cuisine has carved out a strong presence, with wood-fired pizza ovens, handmade pasta, and gelato becoming familiar comforts to locals and visitors alike. Chefs trained abroad have opened refined dining spots where regional ingredients are elevated with international techniques, leading to menus that might feature duck confit with plum sauce alongside truffle risotto or smoked eggplant puree. French influence is also notable, particularly in the café scene, where croissants, éclairs, and tarte tatins are served alongside artisanal coffee in sun-drenched garden terraces.

Asian cuisine has grown in popularity as well. Sushi has become a staple of Chisinau's dining life, with sleek lounges offering extensive sushi menus, dim lighting, and curated cocktail lists. Korean, Chinese, and Thai options are also available, with several establishments sourcing authentic ingredients and maintaining traditional cooking methods. Meanwhile, the growing population of foreign students and expatriates has contributed to an expanding palate for Indian and Middle Eastern dishes. Falafel wraps, butter chicken, kebabs, and hummus platters are no longer rare but integrated into the broader dining culture of the city.

Vegetarian and vegan options have seen a quiet but steady rise. As Moldovan agriculture naturally yields an abundance of fresh vegetables, grains, and legumes, restaurants have begun reimagining traditional dishes without animal products, while international eateries offer modern plant-based menus that appeal to a younger, health-conscious demographic. Organic cafes and juice bars are appearing more frequently, especially in university areas and near major parks.

As evening descends, Chisinau's nightlife begins to stir, offering a variety of options for those eager to explore the city after dark. The local bar scene is diverse and laid-back, with options for quiet conversation, live music, or high-energy dance floors. Cozy wine bars are among the most popular venues, often housed in cellars or tastefully restored historic buildings. These intimate settings showcase Moldova's finest wines by the glass, paired with cheese boards, charcuterie, or light Moldovan tapas. Knowledgeable staff guide guests through curated tastings, offering insights into varietals like Fetească Albă and Rara Neagră.

Craft beer has also found a niche in Chisinau, with microbreweries and beer pubs bringing local flavor to the global trend. Locally brewed IPAs, stouts, and lagers are served in casual spaces with exposed brick, communal tables, and rotating food trucks or street food menus. Some venues host live acoustic sessions or quiz nights, making them ideal for mingling and relaxation.

For those in search of more high-energy entertainment, the city offers a selection of clubs and lounges that stay open well into the early hours. These venues often combine European electronic music, local DJs, and sleek interiors with light shows, cocktails, and a mix of Moldovan and international guests. Popular clubs tend to be found in and around the city center and cater to a fashionable crowd with an appetite for music, dance, and social spectacle.

Traditional folk music hasn't disappeared, however. Certain restaurants and cultural venues host live performances where dancers in national dress perform alongside musicians playing pan flutes, violins, and accordions. These events offer a glimpse into the roots of Moldovan music and are especially popular during holidays or with tour groups, blending entertainment and cultural preservation in a lively, accessible format.

Safety and hospitality define Chisinau's evening culture. While vibrant and occasionally raucous, the city's nightlife is rarely aggressive or intimidating. Most bars and clubs maintain friendly door policies, and while reservations are recommended for upscale venues on weekends, the overall atmosphere remains welcoming. Taxis and ride-hailing apps are readily available, and late-night eateries ensure that the revelry ends with comfort food—often a piping hot plate of *plăcintă*, fresh bread, or fried polenta sticks with cheese.

Dining and nightlife in Chisinau reflect the city's dual personality—deeply rooted in tradition yet open to the future. Whether savoring a home-style Moldovan dinner in a centuries-old cellar, sipping a cappuccino at a Scandinavian-inspired cafe, or dancing the night away in a rooftop lounge overlooking the city lights, the experiences available to travelers are as flavorful and multifaceted as the city itself. This blend of authenticity and innovation defines Chisinau's evolving identity and makes every meal or night out a journey of its own.

Chapter 13: Shopping in Chisinau

Souvenirs and Local Crafts

Modern Shopping Centers

Market Experiences

In Chisinau, shopping is much more than a casual activity—it's an immersive journey into the cultural and social heart of Moldova. Across the capital city, visitors can explore an eclectic mix of traditional craftsmanship, stylish contemporary retail, and vibrant local markets that together tell the story of a place where old-world charm meets the rhythm of modern life. Whether one seeks handcrafted souvenirs, fashionable finds in sleek malls, or the sensory excitement of open-air bazaars, the city offers a distinct and rewarding shopping experience rooted in authenticity and evolving taste.

Handmade souvenirs and local crafts serve as enduring reminders of Moldova's rich cultural heritage. Artisanal creations are deeply embedded in rural Moldovan traditions, where craftsmanship has been passed down through generations. In Chisinau, these traditions are preserved and presented through a wide array of handmade items—each one carrying the character and story of the region it comes from. Embroidered textiles are among the most iconic gifts, often crafted by hand using centuries-old patterns. These vibrant fabrics, which once adorned traditional peasant blouses and home interiors, are now transformed into table runners, cushion covers, and wall hangings that remain faithful to their folkloric origins.

Woodwork is another area where local artisans excel. Intricately carved crosses, icons, jewelry boxes, and kitchen utensils made from walnut or cherry wood can be found in artisan shops and craft markets throughout the city. These items often feature motifs inspired by nature, mythology, and religious symbolism. Pottery, too, holds a special place in Moldovan craftsmanship. Clay jugs, dishes, and decorative figurines reflect both utilitarian function and artistic expression, sometimes painted with earthy pigments and detailed folk patterns. Traditional ceramics from regions such as Cucuteni are especially prized for their historical significance and unique spiral designs.

For those drawn to wearable keepsakes, handcrafted jewelry made from natural stones, copper, and enamel offers a blend of rustic elegance and personal touch. Moldovan artists are known for their ability to fuse ancient symbolism with contemporary aesthetics, creating pieces that are both meaningful and stylish. In addition to jewelry, felted wool products such as scarves, hats, and slippers showcase both warmth and creativity, often incorporating bold colors and floral themes.

Chisinau is home to several boutiques and galleries dedicated to showcasing these traditional arts. One of the most reliable places to explore Moldovan craftwork is the Souvenir Bazaar near the National Museum of History. Here, vendors gather to offer a curated selection of handmade goods, from embroidered linens and carved icons to folk instruments and glasswork. This intimate market is a treasure trove for those seeking authentic, locally made items that reflect Moldova's identity with sincerity and pride.

While traditional crafts speak to the soul of the country, modern shopping centers reflect its contemporary aspirations and increasingly global outlook. Chisinau has embraced the rise of large-scale commercial developments, and the city's modern malls now offer a convenient and polished environment for fashion, technology, entertainment, and cuisine. These centers are more than places to shop—they are hubs of social life where residents gather, families spend weekends, and visitors enjoy a curated blend of local and international brands.

Shopping MallDova, one of the largest and most established malls in the capital, offers a wide selection of clothing, electronics, beauty products, and accessories. With its clean design, climate control, and multilingual signage, it provides a stress-free environment for browsing and buying. The mall hosts familiar global brands alongside popular Eastern European labels, giving shoppers a varied range of choices. Restaurants and cafes inside the mall cater to both quick bites and leisurely meals, while a multiplex cinema and children's play areas make it an all-day destination for many families.

Another notable development is Atrium Shopping Center, situated near the central train station. This five-story complex merges fashion, lifestyle, and leisure under one roof. Known for its trendy clothing outlets and tech stores, Atrium attracts a younger demographic and often serves as a gathering place for students and professionals alike. On the top floor, rooftop cafes and bars provide panoramic views of the city, making it a pleasant place to unwind after a few hours of retail therapy.

Zity Mall, though slightly farther from the city center, is a favorite for those seeking a modern and spacious shopping experience with an emphasis on design and ambiance. The mall features both local Moldovan designers and international labels, particularly in the realms of fashion, cosmetics, and home décor. It also regularly hosts seasonal events and exhibitions, turning shopping into a cultural experience. These malls, with their escalators, polished floors, and international branding, contrast sharply with the city's more traditional markets, yet both types of venues coexist to serve different needs and preferences.

Chisinau's open-air markets, meanwhile, offer an entirely different atmosphere—raw, colorful, and bursting with life. Central Market, or *Piața Centrală*, is the largest and most iconic of them all. Located just a short walk from the city center, this sprawling maze of stalls and counters stretches across multiple city blocks. Its energy is palpable, from early morning when farmers and traders set up their wares, to midday when shoppers haggle over prices for everything from fresh produce to secondhand clothing.

This market is where Moldova's agricultural heritage comes vividly alive. Stalls overflow with ripe tomatoes, fragrant herbs, glossy eggplants, and jars of homemade pickles. Seasonal fruits—grapes, plums, cherries, and watermelons—are sold directly by the growers. Cheese counters offer traditional varieties like *brânză de oi* (sheep cheese) and *cașcaval*, while cured meats and smoked fish add to the olfactory tapestry. Honey from village beekeepers, nuts and dried fruits, and an array of herbal teas tempt those looking for natural wellness products. Sampling is common, and conversations with vendors often lead to warm smiles and helpful tips.

Beyond food, the market has sections dedicated to textiles, shoes, electronics, and household goods. An entire avenue is devoted to flowers, where bursts of roses, tulips, and lilies create a moving landscape of color and fragrance. For many travelers, the Central Market is not only a place to buy—it's an essential part of understanding how daily life functions in the capital. It reveals what people eat, wear, and value, all within a dynamic and democratic space where every transaction is also an interaction.

Smaller neighborhood markets such as *Bazaarul Dacia* or *Piața Botanica* provide similar experiences on a more localized scale. These venues are particularly good for those seeking to avoid the bustle of the Central Market while still enjoying the charm of direct buying. Whether looking for hand-stitched doilies, Soviet-era collectibles, or simply a kilogram of freshly picked strawberries, the markets of Chisinau offer an unfiltered window into Moldova's daily rhythm and enduring sense of community.

Altogether, shopping in Chisinau provides a layered experience that mirrors the city's own character—rooted in history, responsive to the present, and open to the future. In its souvenir stalls, malls, and markets, one finds not only material goods but also moments of connection, discovery, and cultural exchange. These encounters, whether forged over a price negotiation or a shared appreciation for embroidery, create a lasting impression that goes far beyond any object bought or sold.

Chapter 14: Essential Information and Resources

Emergency Contacts and Useful Numbers

Internet Access and Communication

Local Customs and Etiquette

Chisinau, Moldova's capital, offers a travel experience that is rich in culture, warmth, and discovery, but like any international destination, it requires some practical awareness to ensure a smooth and enjoyable visit. For travelers, knowing how to navigate emergency situations, staying connected digitally, and understanding the social customs of the city are just as crucial as knowing where to dine or what landmarks to visit. These essential aspects help create a more immersive and respectful experience while offering peace of mind through informed preparation.

In any city, having access to reliable emergency contacts is critical. Chisinau, as the heart of Moldova's governance and infrastructure, has a well-established emergency response system in place. While services may vary slightly in speed and language accessibility compared to Western European standards, they are generally dependable and increasingly responsive to the needs of international visitors. The universal emergency number in Moldova is 112, and it connects callers to police, fire services, and medical emergencies. Operators may not always speak English fluently, so having a basic phrase or two in Romanian—or using a translation app—can be helpful in urgent situations.

For medical assistance, visitors are encouraged to seek help at larger, centrally located hospitals or clinics, many of which offer emergency services and employ English-speaking staff. Among the more reputable medical facilities in Chisinau are the Republican Clinical Hospital and the Medpark International Hospital, the latter being a private institution known for its modern equipment and multilingual personnel. Pharmacies are widely available throughout the city and are typically open from early morning until late evening. Some central pharmacies offer 24-hour service, and many pharmacists are able to provide advice in English or Russian.

For issues related to lost or stolen passports, legal trouble, or urgent travel document needs, embassies and consulates in Chisinau can provide essential assistance. While Moldova does not host embassies for every nation, several European, American, and Asian countries are represented in the capital. It is recommended that travelers have their embassy's contact information saved both digitally and in hard copy before arriving. In addition, the police can be reached directly for non-life-threatening situations at the number 902, and tourists reporting thefts or disturbances can visit local police stations, where officers are generally courteous and willing to help.

Maintaining communication while traveling is another key component of a well-organized trip. Fortunately, internet access in Chisinau is not only widely available but also impressively fast and affordable. The city boasts one of the best internet infrastructures in Eastern Europe, with widespread fiber-optic networks and 4G LTE coverage. Free Wi-Fi is commonly available in hotels, cafes, restaurants, shopping malls, and even some public parks. Speeds are sufficient for everything from casual browsing to video conferencing, making it easy for travelers to stay connected with friends, work, or digital travel tools.

For those needing constant access to mobile data, purchasing a local SIM card is a simple and cost-effective solution. Moldova's primary telecom providers—such as Moldcell, Orange, and Unite—offer prepaid SIM cards with generous data packages. These are available at kiosks, mobile shops, and airport outlets, and activation is generally quick and hassle-free. A passport is usually required to register the SIM, a standard practice in many countries. Once installed, local numbers allow for cheaper domestic calls, easier restaurant or taxi bookings, and full access to local apps and digital services. International roaming is available for most foreign SIMs, but the rates are significantly higher than those offered locally.

Popular communication apps like WhatsApp, Viber, and Telegram are widely used among Moldovans, particularly for voice calls and messaging. Social media platforms such as Facebook and Instagram are heavily integrated into local social life, and most businesses maintain updated profiles for quick customer engagement. English-language support is increasingly common on local websites and service platforms, especially in the tourism and hospitality sectors, though Russian and Romanian are still the dominant languages in day-to-day communication.

As in many Eastern European cultures, Moldova places a high value on social etiquette and interpersonal respect. Understanding local customs helps bridge cultural gaps and fosters more meaningful interactions with residents. The Moldovan people are known for their hospitality, warmth, and humility, and visitors who reciprocate with politeness and openness are often met with sincere kindness. When greeting someone for the first time, a firm handshake and eye contact are customary, particularly among men. In more familiar settings or between women, a cheek kiss or hug may be used as a sign of affection and camaraderie.

Dress is typically modest and stylish, especially in urban settings. While there is no formal dress code, it is considered respectful to dress neatly in public, particularly when visiting churches or government institutions. Revealing or overly casual attire may be frowned upon in certain places, though the atmosphere is generally relaxed and nonjudgmental.

Dining etiquette reflects Moldova's strong cultural emphasis on food as a symbol of community. When invited to a Moldovan home, it is customary to bring a small gift—flowers, wine, or sweets are especially appreciated. Guests are often offered food and drink in abundance, and it is considered polite to accept at least a small portion. Complimenting the host's cooking is always welcome, and leaving a completely empty plate may be seen as a sign that more food is expected. Table manners are fairly conventional: wait to be seated, begin eating only when invited, and avoid resting elbows on the table.

In conversation, Moldovans may initially appear reserved but tend to open up quickly with warmth and curiosity. Topics like family, history, and culture are well received, while political or controversial subjects are best approached with care unless the person has signaled openness to such discussions. While the majority of the population identifies with Orthodox Christianity, religious diversity is respected, and churches are visited not only for worship but also for their historical and architectural significance. Modest attire and quiet demeanor are expected inside religious buildings.

One unique cultural feature of Chisinau is the dual linguistic presence of Romanian and Russian. While Romanian is the official language, Russian is widely spoken and often used in informal settings. Travelers should not be surprised to hear both languages used interchangeably, and English proficiency is growing, especially among younger people and in the service industry. A few basic Romanian phrases—such as *bună ziua* (hello), *mulțumesc* (thank you), and *vă rog* (please)—can go a long way in making a positive impression and receiving helpful assistance.

Tipping is appreciated though not strictly mandatory. In restaurants, rounding up the bill or leaving around 10% is customary for good service. Taxi drivers do not expect tips, but rounding up to the nearest leu is a common courtesy. In hotels, small tips for porters or housekeeping staff are appreciated and considered thoughtful rather than obligatory.

Overall, the balance of preparedness, cultural sensitivity, and open-minded engagement greatly enhances the travel experience. Chisinau is a city that rewards respect with warmth and offers a high level of safety and convenience for those who approach it with awareness and adaptability. Whether navigating its emergency services, logging on to its fast internet, or sharing a meal with locals, the foundations of a successful journey lie in the small, thoughtful details that help connect visitors with the city in authentic and enduring ways.

Index

A

Accommodation Options – Chapter 11
Apartment Rentals – Chapter 11
Architectural Highlights – Chapter 7
Arriving in Chisinau – Chapter 3

B

Bars, Pubs, and Clubs – Chapter 12
Best Times to Visit – Chapter 2
Botanical Garden – Chapter 6
Budgeting for Your Trip – Chapter 2
Budget-Friendly Stays – Chapter 11

C

Capriana Monastery – Chapter 10
Chisinau History – Chapter 1
Chisinau Landmarks – Chapter 4
Chisinau Parks – Chapter 6
Chisinau Transportation – Chapter 3
Condrita Monastery – Chapter 10
Culture and People – Chapter 1
Cuisine (Traditional) – Chapter 12
Customs and Etiquette – Chapter 14

D

Day Trips – Chapter 9
Driving in Chisinau – Chapter 3
Dining Options – Chapter 12
Discovering Local Markets – Chapter 7

E
Emergency Contacts – Chapter 14
Entry Requirements – Chapter 2
Ethnography and Natural History Museum – Chapter 5
Essential Travel Info – Chapter 14
Exploring the Old Town – Chapter 7

F
Festivals (see Culture and People)
Forests Near Chisinau – Chapter 10

G
Guesthouses – Chapter 11
Grand National Assembly Square – Chapter 4

H
Hiking Trails – Chapter 10
History Museum – Chapter 5
Hotels – Chapter 11
Hidden Gems – Chapter 7

I
Immersive Culture – Chapter 5
Internet Access – Chapter 14
International Dining – Chapter 12

L
Local Crafts and Souvenirs – Chapter 13
Local Markets – Chapter 7

M
Milestii Mici Winery – Chapter 8
Modern Shopping Centers – Chapter 13

Monasteries – Chapters 9 & 10
Museums – Chapter 5

N
Nativity Cathedral – Chapter 4
National Theatre of Opera and Ballet – Chapter 5
Nature Trails – Chapter 10
Nightlife – Chapter 12

O
Old Town – Chapter 7
Opera and Ballet – Chapter 5
Orheiul Vechi – Chapter 9

P
Parks and Gardens – Chapter 6
Planning Your Trip – Chapter 2
Practical Information – Chapters 1 & 14
Public Transport – Chapter 3

R
Renting a Car – Chapter 3
Rose Valley Park – Chapter 6

S
Shopping in Chisinau – Chapter 13
Souvenirs – Chapter 13
Soroca Fortress – Chapter 9
Stefan cel Mare Central Park – Chapter 6

T
Tipova Monastery – Chapter 9
Traditional Cuisine – Chapter 12

Transportation – Chapter 3
Triumphal Arch – Chapter 4

V
Valley of Roses Park – Chapter 6
Visa Requirements – Chapter 2
Visiting Wineries – Chapter 8

W
Wine Country – Chapter 8
Wi-Fi and Connectivity – Chapter 14

Printed in Great Britain
by Amazon